Get it Delivered ☺

Print information available on the last page.

To order additional copies of this book, contact
Partridge India
000 800 10062 62
orders.india@partridgepublishing.com

www.partridgepublishing.com/india

Contents

1

About Author

Atit Purani is a Co-founder and CTO of Space-O Technologies. He ensures software deliveries and leading the technology wing of the organization from the front since its inception in 2010.

He has total 14+ years of experience in Software development in different technologies including Microsoft Technologies, SQL Server and especially around 5+ years in mobile development. Prior to starting Space-O, he worked as Department head for mobile and web division- handling a large team of developers and delivery of Projects on the floor in past employment.

Atit masters his skill of delivery by interacting a large number of offshore clients across the world, understanding their need and psychology and getting things done with a huge number of team members.

The motto that he believes in is – "Focusing on Solutions rather than discussing Problems". Success always comes with hard work, self-confidence and perseverance and it's always better to Win People rather than defeating them ☺

- Someone, who wants to take "pragmatic" approach to successful and happy Project delivery.
- Someone, who wants to excel himself in delivery of Projects.
- Someone, who is taking on a project in his or her home or leisure environment.

Delivery has always been my passion most of my life & I have worked for getting those Projects delivered successfully or making them success by applying delivery rules. During my long career, I have always taken a pragmatic approach to managing projects that do focus on the objectives, which ultimately apply less administration while delivering projects.

As the core theme of this book is "Delivery of Software Projects" it can be primarily used for projects within your own work and even your personal work also not limiting it to IT world.

As the title suggest that the aim is to make the delivery of a Project it should always be "happy" experience". This is achieved by following the rules that during the delivery apart from the routine principles and practices usually people take care off.

We know a lot of things are Project life cycle, planning, building, stabilizing, testing, deploying and signing off the Projects but the real trouble starts during the time of delivery and that is the most crucial phase of Project where if that does not handle properly then there are most chances that Project gets failed.

Get it Delivered, is a summary of my total 14 years of experience in Delivering different Software Projects in my career mostly in agile methodology.

Project Delivery = Getting things done at right time = Happy Customers with value addition ☺

3

This book is dedicated to

"To my daughter who taught me to be patient and teaches me to take Pleasure from small things of Life. Also to my wife and parents who stayed with me in every situation and supported me and most importantly they always believed in their own values given to me."

I would like to thank all my team members and colleagues at Space-O, who gave me all the reason to write this book. Last but not the least, to all my dear friends, past colleagues and everyone around me, who gave me a reason to live in good company.

Lastly, I would like to thank all the people who have contributed directly or indirectly in helping and guiding me.

Thank you all for your wonderful contribution.

4

What is "Software Delivery" & why it is so much emphasized?

Software project management is the art and science of planning and leading software projects. It is a sub-discipline of project management in which software projects are planned, implemented, monitored and controlled. The normal software development life cycle known as SDLC consists of following See image 4.1 below explaining the same.

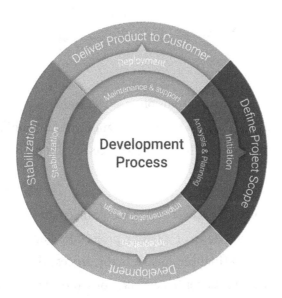

Dictionary meaning of "Delivery" means transporting goods from source to destination. In this context, we can define "Software Delivery" as an iterative process consisting of several transitions & process and finally reaching to the end or we may call the "destination" of Project Life cycle.

If you see below image 4.2, we can clearly visualize that Software delivery starts after Requirements are gathered by business team and it is ready to go into planning phase as shown below.

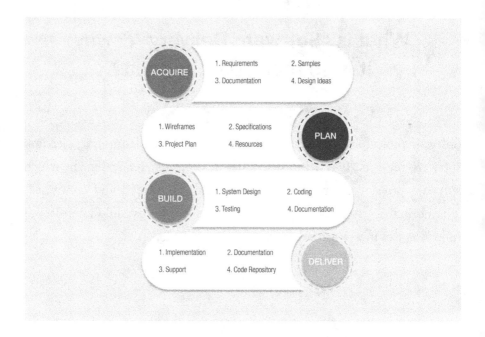

It is the outcome or the final solution as per customer's expectation, which will be either in terms of website, web application, mobile application, software documentation or it may be service fulfillment which client has visualized.

In other words, Software Delivery is the whole mechanism, which comprises of various process and phases of software project development life cycle that ultimately results in a final product. It is the process that gives the desired output to the customer as per his expectations and as per agreement made with him.

To conclude we can say that, Software Delivery of Project is the final process that defines the success or failure story of the Project.

Important Statistics to look at:

According to the Standish Group, a Massachusetts-based consultancy, which is a primary research advisory organization that focuses on software project performance since 1995, released the following data collected over the past 2 decades. These finding updated until 2009, reported the success rate of software project under 3 categories: Succeeded, Challenged and failed.

Project Outcome	1994	1996	1998	2000	2002	2004	2009
Succeeded	16%	27%	26%	28%	34%	29%	32%
Challenged	53%	33%	46%	49%	51%	53%	44%
Failed	31%	40%	28%	23%	15%	18%	24%

Explaining the present trend regarding the high incidence of software failure, Jim Johnson, Chairperson of the Standish Group, further said that the average software project runs 222% late, 189% over budget and delivers only 61% of the specified functions. Evidence suggests little has changed since then.

Further to above statistic, the report elaborated on the success or failure of Software projects under 3 main categories – Software Project Success Factors, Software Project Challenged Factors and Software Project Impaired

Factors and below are the findings:

Software Project Success Factors	Software Project Challenged Factors	Project Impaired Factors
User Involvement (15.9%)	Lack of user input (12.8%)	Incomplete Requirements (13.1%)
Executive Management Support (13.9%)	Incomplete Requirements & Specifications (12.3%)	Lack of User Involvement (12.4%)
Clear Statement of Requirements (13.0%)	Changing Requirements & Specifications (11.8%)	Lack of Resources (10.6%)
Proper Planning (9.6%)	Lack of Executive Support (7.5%)	Unrealistic Expectations (9.9%)
Realistic Expectations (8.2%)	Technology Incompetence (7.0%)	Lack of Executive Support (9.3%)
Smaller Project Milestones (7.7%)	Lack of Resources (6.4%)	Changing Requirements & Specifications (8.7%)
Competent Staff (7.2%)	Unrealistic Expectations (5.9%)	Lack of Planning (8.1%)
Ownership (5.3%)	Unclear Objectives (5.3%)	Didn't Need it Any Longer (7.5%)
Clear Vision & Objectives (2.9%)	Unrealistic Time Frames (4.3%)	Lack of IT Management (6.2%)
Hard-Working, Focused Staff (2.4%)	New Technology (3.7%)	Technology Illiteracy (4.3%)

To summarize, I will put it like below:

"Beyond Software engineering, its Value engineering" – this is very inspiring to me as we always emphasize on SDLC, communication, technology, execution – getting things done etc. and all these are parts of Software engineering to a large extent but there is Value engineering beyond software engineering and that is the actual outcome expected out of Project or Software Delivery. If there is no value addition to the client either in terms of concept, design, presentation, product, communication, promotion, marketing etc. then ultimately it is a failure in the broader world.

Agile Software Management Technique

Since in my all experience dealing software world, I have worked mostly with Agile Methodology, so let me take you through it.

Word "agile" it self-means move quickly with ease. Similarly, if we have to define Agile Software Technique in very easy words then it can be defined as, **"alternative to traditional project management which requirements and solutions evolve through collaborative efforts of team"**. Agile Technique is an alternative to the waterfall or traditional sequential development.

Agile methods principally divide tasks into small incremental builds in an iterative way and each iteration involves cross-functional teams working simultaneously in areas like planning, requirements analysis, design, coding, unit testing, and acceptance testing etc. and working software build is delivered after each iteration with progress in terms of features.

Here is a graphical illustration of the Agile Model:

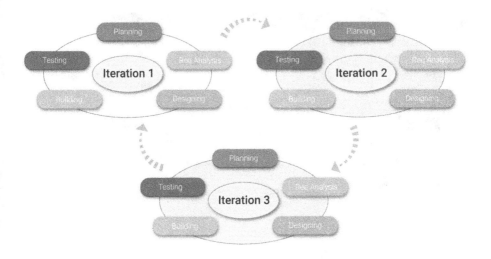

Major difference between agile methodology and traditional models: Agile is based on the adaptive software development methods whereas the traditional SDLC models like waterfall model are based on predictive approach.

Following table lists out the pros and cons of Agile Model:

Pros	Cons
Is a very realistic approach to software development	Not Suitable for handling complex dependencies
Promotes teamwork and cross training	More risk of sustainability, maintainability and extensibility.
Functionality can be developed rapidly and demonstrated	An overall plan, an agile leader and agile PM practice is a must without which it will not work.
Resource requirements are minimum	Strict delivery management dictates the scope, functionality to be delivered, and adjustments to meet the deadlines.
Suitable for fixed or changing requirements	Depends heavily on customer interaction, so if customer is not clear, team can be driven in the wrong direction.
Delivers early partial working solutions	There is very high individual dependency, since there is minimum documentation generated.
Good model for environments that change steadily	Transfer of Technology to new team members may be quite challenging due to lack of documentation
Minimal rules, documentation easily employed	
Enables concurrent development and delivery within an overall planned context	
Little or no planning required	
Easy to manage	
Gives flexibility to developers	

5

Core Software Project Delivery Rules

5.1 Set the Path and framework of Project Execution

5.2 Always make communication clear with clients at the start & end of the Project

5.3 Divide the Project Plan into parts

5.4 Be with your team members and motivate them at difficult point of Project Phases

5.5 Address problems upfront with all stakeholders: team and client rather than waiting for outcome

5.6 Set clear expectations with accountability for each one involved -team members and client

5.7 Make frequent communication at the time of Project completion or deployment

5.8 Acknowledge each other during the last phases of delivery

5.9 Take client approval on completion of each module or milestones

5.10 Training and knowledge sharing of the Product should be given to Client from time to time

5.11 Always have backup plan or configured buffer for development plan

5.12 Recording Project's progress with estimated timelines & cost at regular intervals or at measurable events like completion of phase or milestones

5.13 Testing or checking the quality, performance, or reliability of the Product

Let's start looking at each of the above-mentioned rules in details and try to understand it better. The case study given after each of the rule will explain the real project scenarios, which I have encountered while dealing with different Software Projects with different clients across the world.

5.1 Set the Path and framework of Project Execution

At the starting of the Project from understanding requirements, defining communication method, daily update routine, file sharing, escalation and expected delivery phases in set milestones.

This is the first and most important rule of Project Delivery life cycle. Setting clear path and framework for Project execution is utmost required because that will set the motion for Project execution and ultimately that will lead to Project delivery.

It covers lot of important factors like below:

a) <u>Listing and strictly follow to agreed Project flow and SOW</u>

All the agreed Project scope agreements, wireframes, and SOW will be stored here for records as this is the first and important part of the Project because this will be the baseline for development.

It is also advisable to store the archive of the communication made with the client at the time of Project discussion, which may in the form of chat or voice call because there are many smaller things, which are not documented but discussed at the time of kick-off meetings.

b) <u>Making clear all the technical aspects from both client and development side</u>

Before the start of the development, it should be well communicated and discussed with the client about the technical aspects of Projects like hosting details, Server configuration, mobile devices (with its technical) used in QA, registering for iOS/Android developer account for uploading the apps to respective stores etc. Every small matter should be well defined in advance because many times it happens that at the time of deployment client is not ready with these details that ultimately results in problems.

c) <u>Set realistic timeframes with deliverables</u>

Defining features those are going to be delivered in defined timelines. The timelines should be actual and realistic in delivery phase because many times it happens that timelines, which are given at the initial stages of inquiry or sales, are not accurate because of non-clarity of scope and features. Realistic timelines will help development team to finish the work and it helps client to work on marketing or sales promoting activities those are mostly accurate.

d) <u>Defining clear payment milestones</u>

Once the realistic timelines are set, it should be matched with payment milestones. This is very critical part of the Project delivery because there should be payment synced with every deliverable milestone.

At the time of giving the delivery timeline milestones to the client, it should be 100% clear as what will be payments that are expected by the development team on its approval.

There should be very clarity on payment part as this the core of the Project and any miscommunication can leads to serious problems and ultimately leads to lot of escalations and also Project failure.

e) Setting clear communication channel

Communication is the key to any successful Project so clear communication channel should be set. Clients are 100% aware of who is the developer, designer, QA etc. working on the project if they are communicating with the client.

There should be good knowledge to the client about the Project Manager who is the single point of communication and a responsible guy for delivery of the Project.

Similarly, if there are multiple persons who are going to manage the Project at client side then it should be well defined in advance as who will communicate what and which information development team can get from which of the client Person.

f) Project escalation hierarchy should be set

In the case of any escalation by the client, he should be aware of the Delivery Manager who takes care about all Projects on the floor. It should be well communicated in advance to the client about the top management personnel also if things go out of hands.

This way it gives the client a psychological boost that – "YES" there are top managers and management are in the loop if anything goes wrong and trust me this very important from a client perspective. It also applies to development team also that if there is anything which is not according to plan and set goals then it should be escalated to respective head of the Project or Organization.

g) Making all of them accountable

Roles and responsibilities of all stakeholders of the Project from client and development side should be well defined in advance and once it is defined we can easily make them accountable for tasks they are assigned with.

Once accountability is set, you can get hold of the team member and make them liable for the assigned work or task. Through accountability people are answerable for the end result and in this situation most of them time they perform. So this is the best way to get team on same page and get the desired result.

h) Defining Change request (CR) handling mechanism

A change request is very important in most of the projects that cause the delay in achieving the planned milestones and later on becomes the critical reason for the dispute.

There should be well-defined formula which states that given percentage of scope change (given either in terms of hours or features) will be taken into consideration for given phase or milestone. The client and development team should be well versed with this formula so that there should be clear to both client and team.

In short, if correct Project communication and execution channels are set during the Project's starting phase then it will be the best possible scenario when things go well as planned because everyone is aware about the flow in terms of deliverables, timelines, payments, expected results etc. from starting to end along with clear defined walls with rules of play.

Case Study:

There was a new client coming from Gulf region to our office for his mobile project and I was assigned Project Manager for it. The client had very high expectations as he was in client place and moreover he wanted to see the progress before his eyes as he is here at our office.

When I took over, I understood the requirements from the top view and then arrange a meeting with the client. In my discussions with him, I made clear all the points from above and make a note of it. After that, I met the team and cleared everything with them.

Both my meeting with client as well as team covered all the sub-points discussed above from (a) to (h). This was very important as everyone understood the scope, timeframe, communication, expectations, milestones, escalations, change request etc.

Lastly, when both client and team understood their part, I organized a short meeting and bring everyone one same page. Since both the persons were cleared about an exact path and deliverables, it was much easier for me to manage and get the desired result for the client.

Ultimately, everything worked smooth for the final delivery and client gave us $500 as bonus and invitation to visit his house :)

5.2 Always make communication clear with clients at the start & end of the Project

This is crucial because these are the times when client mostly has hyper expectations.

Communication is sharing & relay of information and facts between people of the organization in an effective and timely manner so that commercial benefit of the organization is achieved. The information can be in the form of data, facts, figures, ideas, feelings, intentions, attitude, expectations, commands or it may be non-verbal gestures, behavior or even sometimes perceptions.

At starting of Project, since the client has not seen any visual progress he is always in a dilemma whether he has selected right team, right people, right platform etc. so always talk to client frequently to set the path and give motion to development.

Similarly, at the closing time, clients again have a lot of anxiety, questions and most importantly lots expectations. In this time, it's advisable for Project Manager of the delivery head to be in constant touch with clients.

Apart from starting and end points, communication should be very clear for daily/weekly updates to client, delay in delivery, delay in response from a client etc. It should be crystal clear and transparent so that all the stakeholders are fully aware of their roles and expectations.

Case Study:

I was dealing with a California client called David for iOS development. Project handover and introduction to each other and team was exchanged smoothly and Project went to development on the floor.

When my Project manager started the conversation with David, he asked a lot of questions from how frequently communication was made, how updates are provided, when calls are made, what is the testing methods we use, what will be next stage once development is done etc. We provided all the necessary information to him. Similarly, when the project was near to finish, the David was very anxious and asked questions daily. He got annoyed on negligible corrections and even got angry few times on slight delay in responding to him.

If you see above example, then you will clearly see that most of the client behave in the same manner as David when Project is in starting scenario when all clients wanted to make sure that everything is correctly understood by development team, all things are in place and communicated, people are responding to them etc. and in another scenario at the time of closing the same anxiety of getting things done as planned and in a timely manner matters the most to any client. They follow you just to make sure that everything is ready for launch.

5.3 Divide the Project Plan in Parts

Particularly for all mediums scale & large scale Projects it is required. Question arises here as why so? Because dividing the delivery into parts helps the development team including front-end guys, database designers, UI designers and QA analyst to focus on particular tasks and finish them within the timeline set.

Similarly, at the client's end, it always good to visualize, test and review the software code in parts instead of seeing it as a single unit. This is more and convenient way to approve the work done.

Mostly we can divide the delivery into multiple parts like below:

-   Initial Understanding Meeting
    Once the Project is in delivery phase, initial kick off meeting should be an important one as this will be the first meeting of the Project with the team and client and making them familiar with each other and basic understanding of the project. This will serve as breaking the ice with all parties.

- <u>Flow and scope discussion</u>
After initial kick off meeting, the Project Manager will discuss the flow and scope of the project with the team and make them aware about the deliverables and expected results from each of them. It will be time when PM should divide the tasks among team members with the discussion of the Project.

- <u>Navigational flow approval with design integration</u>
Once the scope is understood and agreed, design phase starts with the navigational flow of the pages, screens etc with integration of design elements. This is the best stage when client can see the visuals of the work done and get involved into the rhythm. If anything is not according to what is visualized by him then this is the best stage to discuss and get rid of un-clarities.

- <u>Alpha release with integration of basic features</u>
Alpha release is the stage when the application or site or deliverable is ready with most important tasks and features with respect to expected goal. This is the first version which client can see in terms of delivery, which he/she can test and play with.

- <u>Beta release with integration of all functional features</u>
Beta release is the milestone where the application is fully ready to test with all the features and flow integrated as per defined scope and flow except minor tweaks to change or fixing bugs if any in the system. Beta release is always properly tested before it is handed over to client for review.

- <u>Final release before uploading the app</u>
This is the stage when client is reviewing the application for the final time before it gets ready to submit or deploy to respective

platform as per technology and scope. Most there are no changes involved at this stage as it is just for final review and approval.

- Project submission, deployment or closing

  Once app is deployed or submitted to respective platform it is achieved and packaged into folders to be submitted to client. It includes all the properties of Software from source code, designs, documents, formulas etc. After submission is made and acknowledge the Project gets closed officially.

The good example here is that create smaller milestones within your detailed plan that your team can understand and set delivery date for each. This way multiple team members can also work on assigned tasks like designer can work on designs and server guys can work on configuration and setting up database. Don't allow small deadlines to slide and be disciplined and work methodically towards your end goal.

Case Study:

We had an Orlando client named Stephen and his mobile app was related to Pets. Things went very good till the initial discovery and design phase. He was very happy and development was ready to make corrections to get the ball rolling. We also received the necessary payments, which are set for given milestones.

Things started to drift when the beta version was almost ready and client came to us with lot of corrections in design and flow and few new items, which were not discussed at the time of starting the work. The Project managers talked to client about the new things and corrections and even managed to do few corrections but Stephen stick to all the points and which led a big gap between the him and development team and client refused to release the money for this milestone and even exchanged few harsh words.

Our motto was to satisfy client as well as getting the payment for the work done since this was large project and big team was working on the same.

Matter finally escalated to me being the Technical head and immediately I talked to client that I am here to find a win-win situation and not here as a lawyer to fight the case for my team. After successful talk with Stephen, I proposed to divide the pending two milestones into below:

- Pre Beta release
- Beta release
- Final release before upload
- Final release

We agreed on features to be divided on each of the new milestones and also convinced client for CR points. Also, he agreed to divide the payment into new milestones as in his world he is paying for things that are done (psychological impact) in parts.

Ultimately, this whole experience gave me a very unique way to handle the client psychology and achieve the desired results by dividing the big part into multiple parts for delivery that is easy to handle and understand at the client level.

5.4 Be with your team members and motivate them at difficult point of Project Phases

This is the time when team members need more mental and motivational support & guidance by their superior or reporting manager.

When everyone is expecting the results and there are very less chances of errors with one result is dependent on the other, humans are more prone to make mistakes. This is the time when team members of your Project need you (TL/PM/DH). Sometimes they need someone where they can go and relax by just expressing himself or herself and talking to them about their problem or frustration and many times it happens that they are not seeking the solution but they just need the shoulder where they can rely on. The role of leader or Manager here is that of sheet anchor where they can pull the trigger or they can hold the trigger. According to data, more than 50% - 55% of the problems are just emotional and manager being in the role of "Manager", can easily solve it by being with them either by listening to them, motivating them or by guiding them.

Development team needs more mental and motivational support during critical or difficult time of the Project, which is normally during the delivery of milestones or final submission or making the Project live. It has been seen that in last phases of Project completion most of the developers either makes mistakes or surrenders themselves by non-performance or by making mistakes, which they normally do not do and sometimes by emotionally breaking down.

This is the most Critical phase of Project when Leader has to play a key role by staying together with the team, listening to them, making them releasing the mistakes they are making and guiding them to the right direction technically as well as from Project management side. This is the time he has to put in all his experience into practice and get the desired results are not doing it himself but by getting things done from the team. Emotion and motivation play pivotal role in getting things done.

There is no second thought on the fact that people and team can make the project a success or failure so it's always desired and preferred way for every manager or TL or Delivery head to motivate the team when they are in low and non-performing because ultimately its human to make them feel that management and their reporting manager is with them even in bad situation which is tremendously moral boosting for them.

Case Study:

There was a pretty tough time when my team was delivering a Personal endorsement website of one of the Australian Hockey Player. In the last phases of development – client suggested lot of tweaks, which team did and then it was handed over to QA team for final testing.

During this course of time, when team worked on making corrections, bug fixing, quality improvements and in the process of going here and there, they had to stay late nights and work. Sometimes, they have to bear the hard words of client as well as Project manager in finishing the tasks. These whole processes lead to frustration and negativity among 2 of team members. This was obvious as they were working with high pressure and then they have to face the client as well as their reporting manager. This whole incident made them feeling frustrated and personal low.

When I saw these things are happening in my team, I immediately jumped into this situation and talked to my people, spent some time with them, gave them some mental support that me personally and organization is with them, motivate them with good examples and stories and within a day the whole team was again charged up and finish the tasks with the full satisfaction of the client.

5.5 Address problems upfront with all stakeholders: team and client rather than waiting for outcome

During the delivery, it is very important to stay focused and making sure that things are moving as per the plan or not. Any small mistakes or issue can lead to disastrous results in terms of delivery.

Dealing with Problems upfront is the best policy during the delivery as it is also advisable to discuss the problem and get rid of them as soon as possible either by discussing with parties involved forcefully or by making them realize about the problem which it may cause. Delivery is the middle tier where the change in strategy or planning can cause the project to suffer if not handled correctly. So it is always advisable to deal with the problem and find the solution, which according to timeline and scenario is best in the interest of Stakeholders.

There may be many occurrences and situation where problems do arise and it is the responsibility of Delivery head or Project manager to deal with problem(s) upfront. It is always advisable to deal with the problems upfront rather than waiting for the right time because there is no right time when project delivery is divided into multiple phase/milestone and dependent on each other.

If the problem is from development team or with the client it has to be addressed by making sure that it does not affect the overall delivery of the Project. The DH or PM or TL has to be the anchor in dealing with the situation and making sure that problem is handled at the same time it has arise, considering the situation and other factors.

As discussed if that is the problem of the client in terms of change request, slow response or it is the development related problems in terms of non-understanding, wrong calculations, ego problems etc it has been to addressed same time rather than waiting for the correct time because, in Project Delivery, there is no correct time.

Case Study:

If the water has reached the level of neck and if you do not know how to swim then its better to call the lifeguard or someone who can save you until you wait the water to reach the level of your nose.

There was a US client and we were hired to work on mobile app development. Client was not happy with one of the module where we have to load heavy images from server continuously and when it was displaying on mobile app, it behaved very clumsy compared to what is expected.

Team worked on lot of solutions but the end result was not great as there were lot of other parameters involved. Client was obviously not happy with what is shown to his team. Because of this particular feature and displaying image from the server in particular format with customization it took lot of development time.

After checking with our other partner companies also we did not get the exact solution that was discussed in the beginning. Yes, it was a big problem at our part, as we had not anticipated this kind of situation at the time of discussion.

Since the time is going on and frustration level of client was increasing, I had to take the decision of talking straight to client about the problem and told that its not possible to figure out the solution currently and instead suggested alternative way to render and display image. Client was in mood to accept that and told me that my team agreed when we started the Project.

Eventually, I gave the actual picture to client and told him that instead of saying, "Yes" and not getting result, its better to face the problem and work on alternate solution to finish and make the app live. Client agreed and we finished the project which made client not that un-happy which he was during the development phase. If upfront talk with the client was not done then the situation can be slipped out of the hands and may be lead us to cancellation of Project.

5.6 Set clear expectations with accountability for each one involved -team members and client

Accountability is answerability and liability and expectation of account giving. In leadership, accountability is acknowledgement of responsibility or being answerable for resulting consequences for actions and decisions taken by individuals.

When the team is working for set milestone and delivery phases they tend to finish their individual assigned tasks as per plan but if there are no clear expectations set for each of them then it will be difficult at the time of delivery to combine these individual tasks and which can result into a mess.

Without clear expectations it will be very difficult to measure results. Setting up expected results, which are always supported by delivery of features/code within the stipulated time line is required at both ends – clients and development team.

Accountability is the key to successful delivery. There are chances that person does not perform well when they have clear expectations but they are not accountable for their work or actions. It has been seen that mostly all intelligent developers perform well when they are accountable for their deeds. A Person with 100% Clear expectations and who is accountable for their actions can perform more better then person who do this without these two. Once clear expectations are set we can easily measure the results and in case of non-performance or negligence we can take necessary remedial actions.

Since everyone is accountable for their own given tasks there are very less chances of miscommunication and misconception which provides good ground for success. Sometimes it happens that there are inter-related tasks that depend on each other and here the TL/PM or DH has to play the role of movie director where he has to be answerable to both client and development team for each and every action taken place in getting the milestone or task(s) is finished.

Case Study:

Let me explain one interesting and typical scenario I had with one of our European client. She had an e-commerce site and was converting that into a mobile application. We started work in mid of September on tight

Schedule with features fixed as holiday season of November and December was approaching for client.

We finished 80% of the work in the mobile in less then 4 weeks time and by November starting we had the beta version ready to be tested. Suddenly client introduced one more technical person on her side and things started to crumble. He suggested lot of improvement and honestly out of them many are not necessary at this stage of time.

My Project Manager, talked to him and acknowledge it and said that we will finish most critical one at this stage since the season is arriving and we do not want to take any chance but he insisted on making all changes and resulting in lot of corrections at our end and of course bugs with the changes. Technical guy was not testing anything and instead always talks about things we can improve in terms of features, flow etc.

Matter was escalated to me and I looked at whole scenario and arranged a meeting with owner lady. I talked to her that it is not possible to make all the corrections and it is even not practical also considering the Nov-Dec crunch time. I talked to the technical head and set the expectations of just listing the improvement points and discussing & implementing those in Phase-II development. Secondly, I made sure that all those points has to be measured from cost perspective also since making a product better requires funds.

In a client meeting, I made clear that current expectations from the technical person is to make sure that all features and flow is as per the original blueprint or not with checking the technical aspects and approving the test cases generated by my QA team. The same has been communicated to development team that they need to make sure that nothing is left from the original scope and if any bugs are reported, it must be addressed and sorted out soon.

Since everyone was accountable for their tasks the results were good. Client was ultimately happy as mobile app helped to generate more orders for her in the season and later on we were assigned the work for Phase-II development.

5.7 Make Frequent communication at the time of Project completion or deployment

This is the time when client's expectations are at all time high and any miscommunication can lead to disastrous results.

Deployment is the stage where there are lots of iterations happens as this is the final stage of the Project Delivery and of course most the most important one.

This is the thumb rule that development team has to do hyper and frequent communication with client to make sure that all the points and last correction are addressed or not at both ends. If there is anything missing at client end that talk to client and get it clear because it should not be the case when client will say like, "I was under impression that…", "I was not aware…", "I was not knowing this in advance…" etc..

It is a clearly understood that whenever there is statements like above from client, it is a clear indication that problems are ahead. There is a simple psychology that whenever we are near to finish or whenever we are approaching to finish line, we have lot of thoughts and lot of expectations from the outcome so we always tend to be more demanding and more anxious in getting things done and this is the stage when things can go haywire if we do not communicate frequently or regularly.

Always make checklist of the pending items when the app is near to finish and ready for uploading or deploying to live server or submission to client. This is the time when any trivial matter will make the situation worse.

The TL or PM or DH has to make frequent small meeting with the team at starting of each new task or at every 2-3 days to make sure that there is no ambiguity at the understanding level and things are on track. The same applies to have conference call with client to make him understand the current status and also next milestones. You can also talk to client on things we expect from him like feedback on update, details like server credentials, user details, graphics comments etc. The client will also be happy to talk to you on payments as he has all the existing status of the project along with the next expected delivery and milestone data.

Case Study:

It was December end and Christmas was very near after 10 days. Our client Melinda who was working with us for her mobile app for cake recipes was very impatient before the first week of Christmas as she wanted to finish the app and get it lives before holiday's starts in US. Before 2 weeks ago, the situation was different and she was very calm but it changed suddenly.

Technically speaking, there was no problem at the development front but since the App was about to finish and she was very demanding and impatient. She was very furious on minor things and had been upset with the Project Manager, as her expectations were sky rocketed. Suddenly, the matter becomes worst and comes to me being the head of delivery department and within a half hour I understood the situation and send her updates on current situation. At the time of leaving for the day, I also send her email with the things done and things we are working on and I even make sure that I asked her all the necessary things required for uploading which my team need after 2 days time. The next day also, I maintained my system and send her updates 2-3 times a day and even call her once to show the feature working which was actually not at here place.

In the end, the project was finished and the app was uploaded successfully to the App-store before iTunes holidays. She was very happy in the end and even thanked me in the end. But if we see the whole situation then the highlight of her happiness was not me but the hyper communication, which I made with her in the last 3 days. This is human psychology mostly as people get impatient, demanding and even curious on small things when they see that it is near to end because their expectations are very high and lot of other things are at stack once the assignment is over.

5.8 Acknowledge each other during the last phases of delivery

This becomes foremost important and crucial because everyone is busy doing their part of the job and not acknowledging or not replying can lead to serious frustration and unnecessary negativity which impacts the project delivery.

Acknowledgement can be either in terms of express appreciation of thanks, to make the receipt of data/information to sender, to indicate awareness of the fact or situation or it may be to admit or recognize the existence, truth or reality.

At the final stages of delivery, all the parties to the project are working hard to get the delivery and set milestone finished as planned. During this period, many times it happens that we ask for details and also provide details to each other so acknowledgement is very much of importance because since everyone is tied up in their own tasks they forget to ask again, so it's always better to send reply for even small matters because for another one that small matter might be of urgent data or information. Non-replying may result into an unnecessary delay and negativity among team members can lead to delay and may add fuel to failure scenarios.

The Project lead has to play a pivotal role here in coordinating the messages, communication, and tasks between all team members and stakeholders so there is a smooth flow of information to every required person and system. If this has not been monitored or coordinated correctly at the right time then it may lead to serious ego problems among people and which in turn can lead to nonworking, knowing providing false results, low energy on the floor, bad thoughts, negativity etc.

Case Study:

It was afternoon in March and outside temperature was rising as summer was started to show its true color. One of our mobile & web team was working towards the beta release of an app and QA team was involved in testing the data and gave her results in bug tracking tool.

There were a big chaos and lot of arguments in the conference room for discussion with the team. Mobile and Web team had their reasons for each of the bug/tweak identified by the QA. Both the teams were not ready to take the blame on them.

When I intervened and talk to them, I found out that none of them was denying that there were few bugs and no one said that they would not fix it. So I jumped into it and said that since both the team is ready to fix the issues, what is the actual problem. I just take to Project Manager and made him accountable for the situation and said to PM, developers as well as QA that the only problem I see is a lack of communication and not acknowledging each other. Since it was a beta release and all were busy doing their tasks, the Project Manager has to play an important role and making sure that he acknowledges every small request, update, queries etc. to each team, as he is aware of the daily routine.

After 2 days, I observed that work was on track and beta was delivered to client and I saw the missing smile on the face of all the developers including PM. Whenever the Project is in last phase of delivery or any milestone is to be delivered, every small thing should be acknowledged to each other whether it is updates, queries, bugs, logic, design or anything else since it could affect the overall delivery of that milestone, task or Project as a whole.

5.9 Take client approval on completion of each module or milestones

Regular approval from the client on the work done or submitted to them is required mostly through emails after completion of each module or milestone agreed. This is important because in large projects it is very much possible then after finishing few of the modules or milestones there are chances that clients tend to add new features, tweaks in flow and even sometimes changing the designs also.

Sometimes, the team members of the client and development team are changed during the development and this approval and acknowledgment mechanism works for both the parties. It should be practiced that after completion of each module or the set milestones with features implemented it is mandatory for the client to provide email approval that said module is finished and as per decided flow.

This will reduce the chances of friction and argument when there is any feature or change needs to be addressed because during the development both the client and development team will stick to their points, so it's better to have a written confirmation. It is very much in the interest of developers to get the approval from the client for each of the milestones, as it is clear indicator that assigned and planned work is going in right direction. The client will not have any liberty to tell that it is not done or discussed or agreed etc.

Ultimately, it is for the benefit of both the parties because it reduces the points of discussion where there is no agreement.

Case Study:

There was a huge online trading portal we were designing and developing for a South American client. The client visited our office for the signing of agreement and project discussion and understanding.

The project was started and the team finished 2 modules. The client was happy with the progress and then he saw a lot of opportunities outside as he had met with potential customers, investors etc. This lead to a big leap in the app development as he came with a lot of changes and corrections.

Development team listed points and concluded that these points were added in the next phase of development. The client did not like & his frustration was seen in his words as he said that team is not doing a good job, many things are pending in last 2 modules, flow is not stable etc. This was a big surprise for the development team as suddenly the scenario was changed.

They escalated the matter to me and when I observed the situation, I found that there was no written approval by the client for the 2 modules, which were completed. I intervened and after few calls, we agreed on very critical points to be included in current phase and started development. Once it is delivered, I asked client to give us written approval of the things done listing all the features covered.

The client was smart enough and he understood the situation and gave written approval for the modules finished. After that everything was on track as development team had the approval from the client and further development went well with approval from the client for each new milestones making it clear that all that is new will be addressed in next phase of development.

This was a very important lesson for the team as now onwards it is very clear to get written approval from the client on completion of milestone or module to make the future development path smooth.

5.10 Training and knowledge sharing of the Product should be given to Client from time to time

Training & knowledge sharing is an integral part of the Project Completion because ultimately it is the client who is going to use the Product so they should have all the knowledge of Product on how it works and any specification required for its running, maintenance etc. later on.

It has been seen that sometimes the Product is fully functional and up and running but it is the clients who are either not aware about its working or they are not trained or they are not given any knowledge on how it should work. This happens because for big Projects many times, clients are too busy to have a day-to-day checking on features and progress of the Product, multiple partners involved, investors playing their own band in between making the client busy always.

There is no document or demonstration given to client on Product working which can result into Problems because it is ultimately clients who are the final approval authority and since they do not have knowledge about it, they do not agree.

Small training sessions, technical documents, demonstration etc. should be given about the Product, which should include its working, flow and functioning or technical details to clients. This can be given either on every defined milestone or at the end of Product and approval from the clients should be noted down.

Case Study:

My team was developing a mobile application for one of the semi-government department and most of the data needs to be populated from backend admin side. We developed whole of the admin panel and filled it with all the default and existing data available and made the mobile app live. It was typical government scenario where there were a lot of stack-holders and no one was ready to take full responsibility for the application.

I being in the managerial position met my team and we had a discussion about this situation. I told my team to give training of each admin module to client's team members. The purpose was very simple since it had a lot of inputs to be made from admin to get the required output in client mobile app.

Because of the large input to be made in particular sequence, chances are more where operator can forget the steps. And it turned out to be what we expected, client members actually forgot as how to populate and enter the master data to the backend for generating results.

After this, we conducted small training sessions on finishing the pre-beta milestone where we showed them the flow, how entries are made and how to generate the desired reports based on the inputs made by them. We deploy one of our guy to help them to understand everything after completion of every module to make sure that flow is understood by them and this made the path for us smooth at the time of completion as there were few flaws and bugs identified by us which were rectified.

Training and knowledge sharing should be done generally on completion of each module, group of features or milestone. It is very important for clients as that would give crystal clarity to them in terms of application flow and also it reduces the chances of reiteration in final stages of delivery because client and developer both can work on changes and fixes if any at this stage and which is more easy and affordable on time and cost basis too.

Most importantly, when the Project is about to finish, there are almost nothing which is not clear at both ends making the closer faster and ultimately beneficial to the client.

5.11 Always have backup plan or configured buffer for development Plan

All Projects are time sensitive and they have many post-project activities like beta testing and approvals, social media awareness, marketing plans, building sales strategies, advertising etc.

Since every task is interrelated and dependent on each other in a way, delay of one may result in delay of other and ultimately causing the product launching into jeopardy. This is the time when any small mistake can lead to serious problems in the mind of the client(s).

To overcome above scenarios, it is always desired to have backup plans for development that can be in terms of developers working, alternate technology stacks (in some cases), payment cycle and most importantly sufficient gap in timelines.

The better term we can use nowadays is "Configured Buffer for development", which is nothing but sufficient and manageable backup plan for critical areas so that in the case of any emergencies it is managed more efficiently. This way its always in safe hands of DH or PM to measure the performance of Progress and make sure if anything found which is not according to plan then there is opportunity to fix it and work toward the final delivery of Software Product.

Case Study:

We worked on one of our client's website where there were a lot of data manipulations in the form of output generated. Initially, when we designed the architecture of backend server, it was not high-configured one but we anticipated this when we saw that a lot of concurrent users are using the site and we suggested cloud server to the client in between the beta and final release of the site.

It took some time for us to convince client but we managed to change the high configuration cloud server at right time. We were lucky to take this decision at right moment as we saw the speed and other issues in existing server with number of users increasing day by day.

If we have not done for any backup plan for backend server then managing a large number of concurrent users would have been big trouble for the client as well us being development team.

The same can be for any Project where you need to have a backup plan whether it may be in terms of resources, infrastructure, timeline and some-times even technology. Many times you may face that the resources working on the Project are no longer working with you and you need to engage new resources and in this situation documentation and pre-planning of the project becomes very critical.

Being in the role of Manager, it is very much required to take necessary backup action plan for above-mentioned areas. Having a backup plan is always key when the work requires combination of resources, technology etc.

5.12 Recording Project's progress with estimated timelines & cost at regular intervals or at measurable events like completion of phase or milestones

This is the most important factor in the delivery phase, which emphasis on measuring the actual deliverables with the planned one. According to survey more than 50% of the total Software Projects are either overrun by cost and timelines.

It is advisable to measure the Project progress at major milestone with their planned results mainly in terms of timeline, expected data and cost involved. Any Projects which do not measure the results at given intervals are prone to failure as cost and timelines are the main factors which affects both the client and development team and not matching can lead to serious problems at both ends.

If the client is not happy with the timeline and results, then he will pressurize the development team and vice versa the Delivery Manager and management will squeeze the team if cost is overrun + timelines compared the actual one which ultimately passes to the client and result is conflict.

The delivery head or Project manager needs to have a process and documentation method whereby at every major milestone, the delivery is compared with the planned results. This is a good way to perform better since the team is aware of the missing points and they can always fix those points and produce better results which in turn can run into successful delivery at the end of the session.

Last thing here to discuss is that People generally provide estimates in units of calendar time but it's always preferable to estimate the effort (in labor-hours) associated with a task, then to translate the effort into a calendar-time estimate. Sometimes a 30-hour task might take 3.5 calendar days of nominal full-time effort, or 3 exhausting days. However, it could also take a week if you have to wait for critical information from a customer or stay home with a sick child for two days so this is very critical and understood clearly.

Case Study:

I had to deal with this typical scenario. One of the websites Project was going on for an Australian client. It was a website of very popular Australian hockey player where it had a lot of internal pages with quite a few navigations.

The Project Manager working on this Project left in between due to some unavoidable reasons and the Project was assigned to me. After the first instance of submission done by me immediately after taking over the Project, client was furious and angry like anything.

When I looked into details, I found that the problem was due to few reasons but the main reason being the lack of documentation or notes which recorded the progress of the project and its comparison with the planned one.

The old PM did not compare the milestone with the planned one and there was nothing that gave me the clear picture to look at. When I send the new update, the client was furious, as the entire last given feedback was not incorporated along with few corrections, which agreed to be made in the new update. Finally, after talking to the client and taking him into confidence all the pending items are handled and delivered to the client.

5.13 Testing or checking the quality, performance, or reliability of the Product

Testing is the last and very critical part of Software Delivery. It is a process that measures the correctness, completeness, and quality of the developed software or product.

Software testing is an activity to check whether the actual results match the expected results and to ensure that the software system is defect free. If it does not meet the desired results then it turns out into the loss of a client, damage to business reputation, loss of money and time and sometimes resulting in the legal issue for the organization.

There are many tools and techniques & types available for software testing and based on project size, budget, time & requirements, it is used and applied to existing software.

Testing is required at every stage when it is presented to customer for review whether it is initial or interim build or final product. Every piece of the code and module needs to be checked for its functionality, correctness in flow, formulas, presentation part etc.

Case Study:

We had Texas based client and we were developing a shopping cart application for him, which had the pretty large scope and many navigations. The project was finished with all the features and functionality and with almost all test cases tested by the team; it came to me being the Project Manager for final review as "third party customer".

When I checked the app, I listed few very minor tweaks and corrections in UI part, which was necessary from client perspective making it more user-friendly and easy in navigation. I discussed the same points to client in my voice call and he was convinced with the corrections and most importantly was impressed and pleased with my suggestions, which is for making the product more usable and we did it without additional charge since those corrections were not part of the original flow but tweaks to make the product better.

Testing is ultimately a final tool, which makes the app complete, and also it's an indirect way to win clients in the long run. There are different kinds of testing which are performed on a product based on the type of product, requirement, budget etc.

Testing is the final rule, which is performed or used for any of the software or piece of code making it declared as an "application" or a "product". It certifies that what is visualized and agreed with the client is being produced by the development team.

6

Conclusion

In a nutshell, these rules will give you different lenses to see the problem which most of the people in software delivery already know.

This book is intended to demystify project management, to help you see it as a pleasure and not a pain and, overall, to have a real sense of achievement by taking a project from a blank sheet of paper to the delivered solution.

If you read above rules carefully, by implementing those into actual practice will make your life easier and resulting into happy you and customers. Individually you can observe that it will really make a difference to your working and its actual results.

The important aspect of implementing these rules is that we have to follow it religiously like a Morning Prayer and at a right time just to make sure that the rest other will follow leading to delivering happiness.

Let's put it in more clear words:

"Get things done at right time and everything else just falls into the place, which ultimately bring delivering happiness".

Early Life of Author

Atit is a Commerce and Law graduate with diploma in business management before he did his masters in Computers. He did not know at young age as what he will do in his life and then he tried his hands at Computers and it worked finally ☺

During his journey of doing a lot of jobs in different areas like teaching computers at educational institutes to personal coaching, selling SIM cards, data entry jobs, blogging for commercial sites. – it gave him immense experience and exposure as what is most important for end customer and what is most important for vendor or person who does this job for customer.

He thinks, it is DELIVERY of good or services that are different for different jobs. However smart and intelligent you are, it does not make any sense if you are not delivering it correct at the right time where and when it is required.

After getting into serious Software field in the year 2002, Atit was able to justify his belief in "Software Delivery" being the key by working at different levels in organization as trainer, as Jr. developer, as Sr. developer, as Team leader, as Departmental head, as Sales person and lastly as Business Owner. Software Delivery is always which defines and defined result-set which is either correct piece of code or expected results in Software Industry.

I strongly believe that Software Delivery is an Art, which is supported by few mathematics rules (rules of delivery). You need to follow basic rules, which can lead to stage where Software Projects become successful. It is an Art because at both the side there are humans involved - which are clients at one end and development team at other. Every human is driven by emotions by smaller or larger extend and it needs to be handled by applying the rules.

If you are popular person in the team or you know how to get things done from your team then by applying the delivery rules (which I have explained in this book), you can get the Successful delivery of Projects. I am going to explain these delivery rules in later part of this book.

"A Project without Delivery is like a boy winking at a girl in the dark. A boy know what he is doing but the girl does not." – Project Delivery is the mechanism by which the successes of Projects are measured.

www.ingramcontent.com/pod-product-compliance
Lightning Source LLC
Chambersburg PA
CBHW061042050326
40689CB00012B/2940